D1379904

WORLD-FAMOUS PAINTINGS

WORLD-FAMOUS PAINTINGS

★

Foreword by
PIETRO ANNIGONI

With notes on the paintings, short biographies
of the artists and lists of principal works
compiled by
ADRIAN BURY, A.R.W.S.
and
CHARLES RICHARD CAMMELL

THE NEW EDUCATIONAL PRESS
LONDON

MADE AND PRINTED IN
GREAT BRITAIN BY ODHAMS (WATFORD) LTD
WATFORD, HERTS

T.258.Q.

FOREWORD

THE pictures in this book represent the art of painting during the last five hundred years—a span of time that covers the great Continental and English Schools from Giovanni Bellini to the present day. During that time nearly all that we know of truly great painting in the western world has been achieved, an achievement that is the crown of civilization. Here, within the covers of one manageable book, we have the hopes and aspirations of men of genius of many nationalities. Whether they were born in Italy or the north, under whatever potentate and social system, one thing is clear. All these artists were bonded together in fraternal homage to an ideal to express to the utmost of their souls' understanding their wonder at creation, and their gratitude for the gift of life.

There is not a picture, old or new, in this volume, that does not approximate to an important work. Many are indeed masterpieces, bringing honour to the lands that bore the artists, honour to the painters themselves, and above all a certain reverence for the spiritual origin of the Scheme of Things. Some of these pictures are religious and remind us of those divine truths without which the world must relapse into chaos. Others are secular, illuminating the truth of human personality and environment throughout the ages. A few are concerned with landscape, the essential poetry of nature. One feels, however, that whatever the subjects and styles in all their diversity, the artists were unanimous in striving to do the best they possibly could, striving for perfection, and conscious of the difficulty in attaining it.

So much love has gone into these paintings that it is not surprising that generations of men and women have requited that love and taken them to their hearts.

In the course of time these pictures, which were the exclusive privilege of the few, have become the cherished property of the many. They now belong to the world, to you and to me and to all those who believe in the great tradition of art as one of the indispensable joys of life.

Do not ask me which is my favourite painting, for among so many great works it would be impossible to choose. In one mood I might like best the picture by one of my own compatriots. In another, something by Van Eyck or Rembrandt, or Velazquez, something from the French School, or your own Gainsborough, Constable or Turner.

Great art has no frontiers. The thoughts of men of genius are universal and approximate to one another in contemplating the beauty and mystery of creation.

May I say, however, that I am not responsible for the choice of these pictures? And if many fulfil my ideals as to what art should be, there are some that do not quite come into that category. This book is intended as a picture-book in the broadest sense of the word. There is nothing in it that the public can fail to understand. In this respect, all the artists have done their duty to humanity as well as to themselves. There is no mystery about the appearance of any of these works. At whatever time they were done during the last five hundred years the message is clear, and they express some truth that every intelligent person can recognize. Therefore, you will not find in this volume any painting that might look better if hung upside down, or requires some equally obscure literary jargon to support its doubtful authority.

The biographical and other notes by my friends, Adrian Bury and Charles Richard Cammell, about these world-famous paintings are a helpful guide as to Schools, subjects and methods, as well as relevant historical background.

Here is a book about art that you should enjoy. To possess it is to own, as it were, a collection of great paintings ever to hand. To know the pictures herein recorded, to take them into one's memory, is to share in some of the noblest aspirations of mankind.

Pietro Annigoni

THE ARTISTS AND THE PAINTINGS

PREFACE

THE hundred pictures here reproduced and described are justly called WORLD-FAMOUS PAINTINGS. This does not mean that they are necessarily the hundred best paintings in the world, or that they are works by the hundred greatest or most renowned artists. Each painting has been chosen because of its excellence and because for some reason of quality it has become famous and generally well-loved.

It will be observed that many great paintings by universally famous artists are not included, but that is only because such a book as this which contains paintings in a variety of styles and periods must be limited in size. Other volumes could easily contain representative pictures by many artists of equal importance or popularity from the Italian, French, Spanish, Flemish, Dutch, English and American schools. Though many of the works reproduced here are undoubted masterpieces, it is not claimed that all the pictures are of equal merit; and a few have been included because they are more popular than great.

In the biographical notes the authors have tried to portray in miniature the lives and personalities of the artists. The lists of their works appended are in no sense exhaustive, but every effort has been made to make them as accurate as possible. It must be remembered, though, that for various reasons, paintings are not infrequently transferred from one gallery to another, so before the reader makes a special journey to view a particular painting it is wise to check beforehand that it is on view at the gallery named.

A. B.
C. R. C.

MARIOTTO ALBERTINELLI

1475-1515

★

THE VISITATION

UFFIZI GALLERY, FLORENCE

FLORENTINE SCHOOL

The Visitation

THIS picture is universally judged to be one of Mariotto Albertinelli's most sensitive and highly finished works. Moreover, here we find very notably the strange affinity of genius between this pleasure-loving painter and his beloved friend, the ascetic Fra Bartolommeo. The dignity and simplicity of this lovely composition, the beauty of youth and age depicted in the two women, are admirable; while their tender affection reflects assuredly the devoted friendship of the two artists.

The theme is the visit of the Virgin Mary to Elizabeth, the wife of Zacharias, as told in the first chapter of the Gospel of St. Luke. Elizabeth, though advanced in years, awaits the birth of her son, John the Baptist, an event announced to her by the Archangel Gabriel, and to Mary the angel has announced the birth of Jesus, conceived of the Holy Spirit. Elizabeth, embracing the Virgin, is herself "filled with the Holy Ghost", hailing Mary with the words: "Blessed art thou among women, and blessed is the fruit of thy womb. And whence is this to me, that the mother of my Lord should come to me? For, lo, as soon as the voice of thy salutation sounded in mine ears, the babe leaped in my womb for joy. And blessed is she that believed: for there shall be a performance of those things that were told her from the Lord."

It is plain from such pictures as this that, for all his love of life and the visible beauty of the universe, Mariotto Albertinelli possessed, in his own way, a deep sense of religion, seeing God in the beauty of His creations. C. R. C.

Reproduced, by permission,
from the painting in the Uffizi Gallery, Florence.

"MARIOTTO ALBERTINELLI was the most intimate and trusted friend of Fra Bartolommeo, almost, we may say, his other self, not only because they were continually together, but also for the similarity of their manner, seeing that when Mariotto gave undivided attention to his art, there was a very close resemblance between his works and those of Fra Bartolommeo." (Giorgio Vasari.)[1]

There was, however, an essential difference between the characters of the two friends. Bartolommeo (called by his intimates, "Baccio") della Porta was contemplative and deeply religious, while Mariotto was jovial and pleasure-loving, fond of "wine, women and song". When Savonarola, the fanatical monk, commenced his crusade against the licentiousness of the times and all the joys of life, and every expression of artistic beauty, Bartolommeo became one of his earnest disciples, and having sacrificed many of his paintings on Savonarola's notorious "bonfire of vanities", embraced a monastic career. The shock to Mariotto, who detested Savonarola's puritanic enthusiasm, was profound. He abandoned painting and opened an inn, which provided the most fastidious gourmets with choice fare and rare wines.

In course of time Fra Bartolommeo was persuaded by his superiors to recommence painting and to devote his genius to the service of the Church. Gradually the old friendship was resumed. Mariotto, weary of innkeeping, sold his tavern and once more took up his brushes. There is something as charming as it is curious in the devotion of this restless joy-loving spirit to the gentle, ascetic monk. More curious still is the fact that the art of the two should develop on parallel lines and remain harmonious to the end. The Friar died in 1517: the date of Mariotto's death is uncertain, being variously given as 1515 and 1520.

C. R. C.

[1] Giorgio Vasari (1511–74), architect and painter, but known today principally for his ten volumes on the *Lives of the Most Excellent Painters, Architects and Sculptors* (*Vite de' più eccellenti Pittori, Architetti, e Scultori*).

PRINCIPAL WORKS BY MARIOTTO ALBERTINELLI

"Madonna Enthroned with Saints,"
National Gallery of Ireland, Dublin.

"Annunciation,"
Academy, Florence.

"The Marriage of St. Catherine,"
Pitti Palace, Florence.

"The Visitation,"
Uffizi Gallery, Florence.

"Madonna and Child with St. Jerome and St. Zenobia,"

"Christ Appearing to the Magdalene,"
Louvre, Paris.

"St. Catherine,"
"The Magdalene,"
Gallery, Siena.

"Annunciation,"
Cathedral, Volterra.

"Virgin and Child with St. John,"
Smithsonian Institute of Fine Arts, Washington.

PIETRO ANNIGONI

1910-

*

HER MAJESTY QUEEN ELIZABETH II

FISHMONGERS' HALL, LONDON

ITALIAN SCHOOL

Her Majesty Queen Elizabeth II

THIS is one of the finest royal portraits done during the present century, and compares not unfavourably with the great classics of royal portraiture.

While conscious of the masterpieces of the past, and having studied them carefully, as all artists must do if they are to develop their own personalities on constructive lines, Signor Annigoni has none the less expressed the theme with a new and inspired feeling for the grace, beauty and dignity of the royal personage that accords with modern democratic sentiment.

It is the youthful Queen on the threshold of the future, looking towards that future with courage and confidence. Wearing the historic Garter robes of royal ancestral origin, Her Majesty is seen, not in remote sovereignty, but as the first Lady of the great British Commonwealth of Nations.

The background, with its feeling for space and air, the suggestion of Windsor Castle in a far landscape with slender trees at the moment of spring, is symbolic of the great reign to be. The portrait is the result of deep meditation and many preliminary notes and sketches that the artist made in the course of sittings at Buckingham Palace. In the bottom left-hand corner is a tiny figure in a boat, which is the artist himself fishing, an unconventional way of signing the portrait.

I remember how moved I was when I saw Signor Annigoni putting the finishing touches to this portrait in a studio at the top of a tall house, facing the Thames, on a summer morning in 1955. The little company of intimate friends of the artist, who had the privilege of the occasion, were all intensely happy that Annigoni had so signally succeeded in what is always a severe test of an artist's responsibility and power—the painting of a royal portrait.

There was no doubt that it was not only a supreme work but likely to be a popular one, and that it has proved to be. I doubt if any other portrait in the history of art has achieved more deservedly universal acclaim. A. B.

PIETRO ANNIGONI was born in 1910 in Milan, the son of a well-known engineer. By the age of six he had shown remarkable talent and his father determined that he follow the profession of art. He first studied at the *Ginnasio*, Florence, in 1925, and at seventeen entered the Florentine Academy of Arts. Working, however, independently of the modern idiom, Annigoni looked at the old masters and, like them, was a great draughtsman before he was twenty. In the intervals of intense work he wandered about Italy, France, Holland and other countries, absorbing the ideals of every established school of painting, selecting what most appealed to his temperament, and making innumerable notes and sketches.

Annigoni also explored the technical methods of the old masters, and adapted them to suit his own style. Several one-man shows in Italy proclaimed his genius in his native country, but it was not until he exhibited his self-portrait at the Royal Academy in 1949 that he became known in England. Here was a work so far transcending the usual run of contemporary portrait painting that it caused a sensation in the art world. An exhibition of portraits and subject-pictures at the Wildenstein Galleries, New Bond Street, set the seal on his reputation.

Annigoni, while being the most celebrated portrait painter in the world, is an artist in the complete sense of the word. His religious pictures and landscapes take up much of his time. At the age of forty-seven, with a tremendous output of memorable work behind him, he can look forward to many years of achievement. He has already had a fruitful influence on the younger generation of artists.

A. B.

PRINCIPAL WORKS BY PIETRO ANNIGONI

Portraits:

H.M. Queen Elizabeth II,
The Fishmongers' Company, London.

H.R.H. The Duke of Edinburgh,
The Fishmongers' Company, London.

H.R.H. Princess Margaret,
Clarence House, London.

Princess Elena Corsini,
Prince Corsini Collection, Florence.

Miss Juanita Forbes,
Miss Forbes's Collection.

Miss Margaret Rawlings,
Miss Rawlings's Collection.

Mrs. Christie Miller,
Mrs. Miller's Collection.

Lord Moran,
Lord Moran's Collection.

Subject-Pictures:

"Harmony in Tuscany,"
Lady Howard de Walden Collection.

"Christ Walking on the Waters,"
Prince Corsini Collection.

"Winter,"
MacMahon Collection, San Francisco.

"St. Francis Talking to the Birds,"
Croff Collection, Milan.

"Say you this is Man,"
Signor Luigi Bressani Collection.

Fresco in the Convent of St. Mark, Florence.

GIOVANNI BELLINI

c 1435–1516

*

DOGE LOREDANO

NATIONAL GALLERY, LONDON

VENETIAN SCHOOL

Doge Loredano

THE Loredano family provided several great men for the Venetian Republic, including Doges, but none could have had a more difficult or critical term of duty than the Doge Loredano, born in 1437. He was sixty-six when elected Doge, and is described by a contemporary as a tall, spare man with massive features, very kind-hearted but passionate, an able public servant but by no means rich, his fortune being estimated at 30,000 ducats.

During Loredano's lifetime, and particularly when supreme head of the state, the fortunes of the Republic were on the wane. Having "held the gorgeous East in fee", Venice lost Constantinople to the Ottoman Turk. Disaster followed upon disaster. The discovery of the Cape route to the east by Diaz in 1486 robbed the Republic of her monopoly of oriental trade. The League of Cambrai, which ranged the European powers and Rome against Venice, threatened her with destruction. The war dragged on, and Doge Loredano in 1513 mounted the tribune and described the critical situation. His Serenity deplored the loss of places so near Venice, and he pressed the need of money to carry on the war. "The public treasury," he said, "is unequal to such expenses. Therefore all debtors to the state are exhorted to pay their arrears." Loredano urged everybody to help with service or money, to discharge their obligations to the Government and curtail their private expenditure. He had sent his own silver plate to the mint.

The enemies of Venice falling out among themselves, the Republic was preserved. But the sunset of Venice as a great power had begun. She was, however, to bask in her glorious memories—military, naval, cultural and mercantile—for another three centuries. Doge Loredano died at the age of 84, five years after the death of Giovanni Bellini.

A. B.

IOANNES BELLINVS

GIOVANNI BELLINI. The Bellini family may be said to have founded the Venetian School of painting. Giovanni was the son of Jacopo Bellini, the brother of Gentile, and the brother-in-law of Mantegna, through his sister's marriage to that artist. Living at a time when the Venetian Republic began to celebrate in art her past magnificence, the Bellinis, father and sons, employed their genius in illustrating its splendours, and collaborated in important works of a historical and religious character.

Brought up in his father's workshop, Giovanni went to Padua in 1548, and was influenced by that school of painting. His early works reveal the somewhat austere style of Mantegna, but as the years passed he acquired a richer colour scheme and warmer sentiment. In 1470 he executed a large design for the School of St. Mark. Towards the end of the 1470's he travelled to Pesaro to work on the great altar-piece, "The Coronation of the Virgin" in the church of St. Francesco, to which period also belongs "The Transfiguration" at Naples. On the occasion of his brother's departure for Constantinople in 1479 to paint the portrait of Mohammed II, Giovanni took Gentile's place as artist to the Ducal Palace in Venice. The altar-piece at Pesaro set the course for many similarly grand religious works. There was the "Madonna and Saints" for SS. Giovanni and Paolo, in Venice, a painting that was destroyed by fire in 1867. He was constantly engaged on works for the Frari, SS. Giobe, Zaccaria and other Venetian churches. Dürer, who knew him, greatly admired his work, and wrote to his friend, Pirkheimer, in 1506, "Everyone tells me what an upright man he is, so I am genuinely fond of him. He is very old and yet he is the best painter of all". Bellini's style influenced the sixteenth-century Venetian School. Two of his pupils were Giorgione and Titian. Giovanni Bellini died in 1516.

A. B.

PRINCIPAL WORKS BY GIOVANNI BELLINI

"Two Venetian Personages,"
National Gallery of Ireland, Dublin.

"The Earthly Paradise,"
Uffizi Gallery, Florence.

"Doge Loredano,"
"The Agony in the Garden,"
National Gallery, London.

"Madonna and Child,"
"Pieta,"
Brera Gallery, Milan.

"Transfiguration,"
National Museum, Naples.

"St. Francis,"
Frick Collection, New York.

"Madonna and Child,"
Metropolitan Museum of Art, New York.

"Christ Blessing,"
National Gallery of Canada, Ottawa.

"Portrait of a Man with Long Black Hair,"
Louvre, Paris.

"Coronation of the Virgin,"
Ducal Palace, Pesaro.

"Virgin and Child with Saints,"
Academy, Venice.

"Madonna and Child,"
United States National Gallery of Art, Washington.

PARIS BORDONE

1500-1571

★

THE LOVERS

BRERA GALLERY, MILAN

VENETIAN SCHOOL

The Lovers

HERE we have a poet's ideal theme given visible form by a peculiarly poetic painter. Though the lovers dominate the scene with that sense of absolute and certain love which the poets of Italy had derived, first from Provence, and later from Plato himself, though, contemplating the picture, we may say with Guido Cavalcanti, "There Love in very presence seemed to be," yet there attaches to this painting another and somewhat disquieting interest, occasioned by the intrusion of the shadowed, bearded figure behind the lady.

Who is this man, and why is he introduced by the artist? Bordone is evidently telling a story familiar to the Italians of his time. Can it be that we have here a Venetian version of the romance and tragedy of Francesca of Rimini and Paolo Malatesta, immortalized by Dante? Does the man in the shadows represent the jealous, vengeful Gianciotto, stealing upon the lovers to slay them? The picture reminds us forcibly of one with the same title by Palma Vecchio: Bordone's picture, indeed, is painted as nearly as possible in Palma's manner. But in "The Lovers" by Palma the figure in the shadows is young and friendly, and may perhaps represent an adolescent Eros. The sinister suspicion which lingers in our minds regarding Bordone's intruder is absent. C. R. C.

Reproduced, by permission,
from the painting in the Brera Gallery, Milan.

PARIS BORDONE. "The artist who has most successfully imitated Titian was Paris Bordone, who, born in Treviso, of parents, one a Trevisano, the other a Venetian, was taken at the age of eight to certain of his mother's kindred in Venice." (Giorgio Vasari.) Of noble birth, he was educated with all the refinements of Renaissance culture, and giving early evidence of a genius for art, as also for music, he was placed under the tutorship of Titian, then in the prime of his splendid career.

Bordone, like other of his pupils, found Titian a careless and jealous teacher, yet he mastered thoroughly the principles of his art. Leaving Titian, he followed with passionate enthusiasm the manner of Giorgione, and studied carefully the works of Palma Vecchio. Thus equipped, he developed a manner of his own, rich with the warmth of Venetian colour, marked with an accent of vigorous individuality.

In 1539 Paris Bordone went to France, where he "painted numerous portraits of ladies" for François I, "with other pictures of different kinds". Of Bordone's extant works the unquestioned masterpiece is the great painting in Venice of "The Fisherman bringing the Ring of St. Mark to the Doge Gradenigo", where the magnificent architectural décor frames the many actors in the ceremony, the whole brilliantly achieved for design and colour.

His latter years Bordone passed in Venice, living "quietly in his own house, working only at the request of princes, or others of his friends, avoiding all rivalry, and those vain ambitions which do but disturb the repose of man". C. R. C.

PRINCIPAL WORKS BY PARIS BORDONE

"Madonna and Infant Jesus enthroned, with Saints,"
Museum, Berlin.

"Holy Family with St. Jerome and St. Elizabeth,"
"Diana and her Nymphs,"
Royal Gallery, Dresden.

"The Sibyl revealing to Augustus the Mystery of the Incarnation,"
"St. George,"
"Portrait of Pope Paul III,"
Pitti Palace, Florence.

"Holy Family,"
Art Gallery and Museum, Glasgow.

"Christ giving Benediction,"
Royal Gallery, The Hague.

"The Light of the World,"
"Daphnis and Chloe,"
"Portrait of a Genoese Lady,"
National Gallery, London.

"The Lovers,"
"The Baptism of Christ,"
"The Madonna,"
Brera Gallery, Milan.

"Man in Black Counting Jewels,"
Bayerische Staatsgemäldesammlungen, Munich.

"Vertumnus and Pomona,"
Louvre, Paris.

"Holy Family,"
Palazzo Colonna, Rome.

"Mars and Venus,"
Palazzo Doria, Rome.

"The Fisherman Bringing the Ring of St. Mark to the Doge Gradenigo,"
"Paradise,"
Academy, Venice.

"The Body of Jesus upheld by Angels,"
Doges' Palace, Venice.

"Venus and Adonis,"
"Allegory,"
"Combat of Gladiators,"
"A Young Lady at her Toilet,"
Albertina Gallery, Vienna.

SANDRO BOTTICELLI

c 1447 - 1510-15

*

THE BIRTH OF VENUS

UFFIZI GALLERY, FLORENCE

FLORENTINE SCHOOL

The Birth of Venus

Botticelli's two most famous paintings of mythological subjects, "The Birth of Venus," and "Primavera," now among the glories of the Uffizi Gallery at Florence, were painted for the villa of the Medici at Castello. The former depicts the legendary rising of the Grecian goddess, Aphrodite "the foam-born" (the Roman Venus), from the sea at Paphos on the shore of Cyprus. The model for this Venus, according to tradition, was Simonetta, the beautiful mistress of Giuliano de' Medici, whose tomb in the Medici chapel in Florence, sculptured in marble, is one of Michelangelo's greatest works.

Walter Pater considered "The Birth of Venus" to be Botticelli's "most complete expression" of that Hellenic vision expressed in medieval terms which was his singular gift: here "the grotesque emblems of the middle age, and a landscape full of its peculiar feeling, and even its strange draperies, powdered all over in the Gothic manner with a quaint conceit of daisies, frame a figure that reminds you of the faultless nude studies of Ingres". Pater reflects on the cold light, the "mere sunless dawn"; but "you can see the better for that quietness in the morning air each long promontory, as it slopes down to the water's edge".

Such paintings are veritably poems, the thought and measure of which have been subtly transmuted into form and colour. They may perhaps be more lucidly described in verse than prose, as thus "The Birth of Venus":

"Using a scallop-shell for coracle,
Blown shoreward by the wind she came to land;
Over her shoulder the long tresses fell,
Whose gold she wreathed about her with her hand;
The waves, who were the first to feel the spell,
Kissed her white feet before they touched the strand;
There Flora wrapped her in a flowery cloak,
And all that's lovely in the world awoke." [1]

C. R. C.

[1] C. R. C.: *The Triumph of Beauty.*

Reproduced, by permission, from the painting in the Uffizi Gallery, Florence.

SANDRO BOTTICELLI. No painter was ever more filled with the spirit of poetry than Alessandro Filipepi, known to fame as Botticelli from the name of a jeweller, Botticello, a friend of his father, to whom he was apprenticed as a boy. His talent for drawing was soon manifest, and Sandro Botticelli, as he was henceforth styled, became a pupil of the renowned painter, the Carmelite Friar, Filippo Lippi.

Botticelli's character is clearly reflected in his art. Whether he painted scenes from Greek mythology or from Bible stories his pictures are all charged with a pensive beauty, delicate, melancholy, wistful. "It is this [says Walter Pater] which gives to his Madonnas their unique expression and charm. He has worked out in them a distinct and peculiar type, definite enough in his own mind, for he has painted it over and over again. . . . Hardly any collection of note is without one of these circular pictures."

The influence of Botticelli on the English Pre-Raphaelites, D. G. Rossetti and Burne-Jones, is obvious.

Half medieval, half Renaissance, his paintings reveal curious defects (like the coarseness of drawing often found in the hands and feet) and extraordinary beauties. Nothing lovelier exists in sacred art than the little Madonna showing an illuminated picture book to the baby Jesus, in the Poldi-Pezzoli collection at Milan; nothing more romantic in conception or execution than "The Birth of Venus" (here reproduced) or the "Primavera"—that other Venus, who presides over springtime—both in the Uffizi.

Like Fra Bartolommeo, Botticelli became a follower of the fanatical Savonarola, who caused a puritanic revolution in Florence. He abandoned painting in despair and fell into pitiful poverty, from which he was rescued by the magnanimity of those supreme patrons of art, the Medici, whom Savonarola had savagely attacked.

Botticelli illustrated Dante's *Inferno*, and his pictures often recall the poet's *Vita Nuova*.

C. R. C.

PRINCIPAL WORKS BY SANDRO BOTTICELLI

"Lucretia,"
"Madonna dei Chigi,"
"Holy Family,"
Gardner Collection, Boston, U.S.A.

"Ecce Homo,"
"Crucifixion,"
Fogg Art Museum, Cambridge, U.S.A.

"Madonna and Child with Angels and Saints,"
Academy, Florence.

"The Birth of Venus,"
"Calumny,"
"Madonna of the Melagrana,"
"Fortitude,"
"Primavera,"
Uffizi Gallery, Florence.

"The Annunciation,"
Art Gallery, Glasgow.

"Adoration of the Magi,"
"Mars and Venus,"
"The Nativity,"
National Gallery, London.

"Madonna and Child, with book,"
Poldi-Pezzoli Collection, Milan.

"St. Zenobius,"
"Magi,"
Metropolitan Museum of Art, New York.

"Adoration of the Magi,"
"Portrait of a Youth in a Red Cap,"
United States National Gallery of Art, Washington.

"Destruction of Korak, Dathan and Abiram,"
"The Temptation of Christ" (frescoes),
Sistine Chapel, Vatican, Rome.

FRANÇOIS BOUCHER

1703-1770

*

MADAME DE POMPADOUR

NATIONAL GALLERY OF SCOTLAND, EDINBURGH

FRENCH SCHOOL

Madame de Pompadour

No painting could express more perfectly the elegance of eighteenth-century France than this one of Jeanne-Antoinette Poisson. Every detail and all the colours are exquisitely organized to accentuate the charm of a woman of destiny. Here are the head and hands that led a nation from one misfortune to another, and helped ultimately to bring about the French Revolution.

Known to history as the Marquise de Pompadour, of dubious parentage, but of singular beauty and wit, she was brought up by her mother to play the rôle of king's mistress. Married in 1741 to Le Normant d'Etioles, nephew of her guardian, Le Normant de Tournehem, a rich man, Jeanne-Antoinette attended the theatre and other social functions in Paris, and soon became a queen of fashion. When Louis XV first saw her at a ball at Versailles he was completely infatuated. Nor was she slow in abandoning her husband for a royal lover.

Pleasure-loving Louis XV was only too glad to allow La Pompadour to relieve him of the problems of state affairs, and before long she was the dominant power behind the throne. For twenty years she ruled or rather misruled France, making and breaking ministries according to her whim. La Pompadour reversed the traditional policy of France because Frederick the Great laughed at her, and brought about the Seven Years War. A cynical and subtle intriguer, she retained her influence over Louis XV for many years. Nor was she above conniving at the king's other love affairs. Something, however, can be said in her favour: she was a lavish and intelligent patroness of the arts, and an amateur artist herself. She took lessons in drawing from Boucher, who painted several portraits of her. She died in 1764, at the age of forty-three.

A. B.

FRANOÇIS BOUCHER, the son of a little-known artist who taught him the rudiments of drawing and painting, entered the studio of François Lemoine, the great decorative artist, and from him learned how to compose wall and ceiling decorations with the alluring gods and goddesses of pagan mythology.

Boucher was soon earning a living in this way, and by his drawings and engravings for books and show-cards, but decided to complete his studies in Rome. His style being already formed, the Roman manner did not appeal to him, and he was not happy there.

On returning to Paris, Boucher worked to such purpose that he was admitted to full membership of the Academy in 1734, after the submission of his picture "Renaud et Armide". When the Salon, which had been closed for some years, reopened in 1737, Boucher's real triumph began, and year after year his pictures were the sensation of the art world.

Boucher also designed tapestries for and became Director of the Beauvais factories. Simultaneously, he was a scenic artist and designed the décor for the opera and theatres. These decorations, like his Salon pictures, were the talk of Paris. His fame increased with everything that he achieved, particularly his voluptuously composed and coloured mythological subjects, such as "The Birth of Venus", "The Bath of Diana", "Zephyr in the Palace of Love", "Sunrise" and "Sunset", with the human figure as their motive.

One of the first things that Madame de Pompadour did when she gained power was to grant Boucher a monopoly for the decoration of royal buildings and residences. The brothers Goncourt in their book, *French Eighteenth-Century Painters*, inform us that Boucher was the painter with whom La Pompadour enjoyed discussing art. He taught her to draw and etch. Whether designs for garden-ornaments, title-pages to books, fountains, buildings, pieces of furniture, Boucher was the artist she consulted. It was due to her that he was appointed chief Court painter in 1765, though La Pompadour had died the previous year.

Not only in France but in Europe generally, as far as Russia, Boucher was the vogue. He was universally admired and *le style Boucher* penetrated into every aspect of eighteenth-century art and craft. There was apparently only one discordant voice, Diderot's, and the great French critic raised it over and over again when he saw Boucher's works at the Salon. "Degradation of taste, colour and composition", said he, with expressions far more abusive in a personal way. But the artist did not care. Easy-going, rich, and prodigiously energetic, even as an elderly man, he was never happier than when at his easel, painting until the daylight went.

Without any boastful intent Boucher declared that he had done in the course of his life 10,000 drawings and painted at least 1,000 pictures. He died in 1770. A. B.

FRANÇOIS BOUCHER

1703-1770

*

YOUNG LADY WITH A MUFF

LOUVRE, PARIS

FRENCH SCHOOL

Young Lady with a Muff

THE Brothers Goncourt write that Boucher, somewhat weary of a bachelor existence, planned to take a wife, and on 21 April, 1733, when the artist was thirty, he married Marie-Jeanne Buseau, a lovely girl whom he had known since her childhood. She was only seventeen when she become not only the artist's wife but the inspirer of many of his "goddesses". Her features and figure are to be identified in the artist's allegorical paintings. An ideal model in every sense of the word, she was also very intelligent and something of an artist herself, and her facility for drawing and painting rapidly improved under her husband's supervision.

Boucher's vast output has always been a matter of wonderment, even though he was recognized as an indefatigable worker. Perhaps his gifted wife helped her husband more than is generally known.

It is an interesting fact that Mme Boucher, immediately after her husband's death, was granted a pension of 1,200 *livres*, in consideration of the services rendered by her husband, and later, when she was old, Louis XVI doubled the pension.

Whether the "Young Lady with a Muff" is Mme Boucher is uncertain. Some experts think it an early study of Mme de Pompadour. Perhaps the portrait is a blend of both. It is obviously the type of feminine beauty that appealed to the artist.

A. B.

PRINCIPAL WORKS BY FRANÇOIS BOUCHER

"Two Figures,"
Jeffries Collection, Boston, U.S.A.

"The Halt at the Fountain,"
"Peace and War,"
Museum of Fine Arts, Boston, U.S.A.

"Bathing Nymph,"
Art Institute, Chicago.

"Mme de Pompadour,"
National Gallery of Scotland, Edinburgh.

"Mme de Pompadour,"
"Venus and Cupid,"
"The Judgment of Paris,"
"Venus and Mars Surprised by Vulcan,"
"An Autumn Pastoral,"
"A Summer Pastoral,"
"The Modiste,"
Wallace Collection, London.

"The Four Seasons,"
"Le Dessin,"
"La Musique,"
Frick Collection, New York.

"Birth and Triumph of Venus,"
"Toilet of Venus,"
Metropolitan Museum of Art, New York.

"Rinaldo and Armida,"
"Diana Leaving the Bath,"
"Young Lady with a Muff,"
"The Forge of Vulcan,"
"The Painter's Studio,"
"The Three Graces,"
Louvre, Paris.

"The Triumph of Venus,"
"The Triumph of Galatea,"
National Museum, Stockholm.

FORD MADOX BROWN

1821-1893

★

THE LAST OF ENGLAND

TATE GALLERY, LONDON

BRITISH SCHOOL

The Last of England

THERE is something intensely moving about this picture, for it expresses to perfection the nostalgic anxiety of two emigrants leaving their homeland to seek their fortune and future in Australia. "The Last of England" was inspired by the departure of the poet-sculptor, Thomas Woolner, Brown having gone to Gravesend to bid him goodbye.

We feel close to these wanderers in their regret at saying farewell to old friends, but we are also fascinated by the costumes of the period—the greatcoat of the man and the cloak of the woman, and that umbrella which as yet survives the force of the wind blowing the hat-ribbon across the man's coat. And how wonderfully effective is that streak of rose-pink in the generally sombre colour scheme. The woman's clasped hands have their part in the sentiment of the picture, as if supplicating the years to come. The small child in the background is carefully drawn and painted, as are the hands of the other emigrants in the background. Ford Madox Brown obviously felt this parting deeply.

The artist wrote, "Without heeding the art of any people or country, I have tried to render the scene as it would seem. I thought it necessary to imitate the minuteness of detail which would be visible in the same conditions of full daylight in order to accentuate the intimate emotion of the subject."

Thomas Woolner was a member of the Pre-Raphaelite Brotherhood and contributed poems to *The Germ*, their magazine. It is a revealing fact that he remained in Australia only about two years, returned to England, was made a Royal Academician in 1874, and Professor of Sculpture there during 1877–9. "The Last of England", therefore, as far as he was concerned, was not "the last", just a temporary phase, but his emigration has been immortalized in one of the best paintings of the nineteenth century.

A. B.

FORD MADOX BROWN was born of English parents at Calais in 1821. He first studied in Bruges, Ghent and Antwerp, under Van Hauselaer and Baron Wappers. After three years in Paris, Brown produced "Manfred on the Jungfrau" and "Parisina's Sleep", in which the artist's dramatic temperament is already evident. Coming to London, he entered the competition for the Westminster cartoons, and carried out one of his designs, "Willemus Conquistator", in 1861, as an oil picture.

Wishing to increase his knowledge, particularly of colour, Brown visited Italy in 1845, and as a result his work much improved in this respect, as may be seen in such paintings as "Wyclif Reading his Translations to John of Gaunt", which is dated 1848. A work of similar character is "Chaucer at the Court of Edward III", which was painted three years later.

Though Brown was not a member of the Pre-Raphaelite Brotherhood, he was sympathetic to their ideals, and there is little doubt that his own sincere attitude towards art stimulated theirs.

A prodigious, if slow, worker, largely on account of the detail and research essential to his religious and historical subjects, Brown's works were conspicuous at a time when the general average of painting in England and Europe was somewhat indifferent. Such pictures as "Lear and Cordelia", "Cromwell Dictating the Vaudois Despatch to Milton", "Christ Washing Peter's Feet", and "Work", in which the portrait of Thomas Carlyle is easily recognizable, proclaim an artist of exceptional feeling and technical power. Ford Madox Brown had just completed a series of twelve frescoes for the Manchester Town Hall when he died on 6 October, 1893. A. B.

PRINCIPAL WORKS BY FORD MADOX BROWN

"The Last of England,"
"The Finding of Don Juan by Haidee,"
"Elijah and the Widow's Son,"
"Work,"
"An English Autumn Afternoon,"
City Museum and Art Gallery, Birmingham.

"The Death of Tristram,"
Fitzwilliam Museum, Cambridge.

"Our Lady of the Good Children,"
"Lear and Cordelia,"
"Take your Son, Sir,"
"The Last of England," (smaller version)
"Christ Washing Peter's Feet,"
Tate Gallery, London.

"Work" (smaller version of the Birmingham picture),
City Art Gallery, Manchester.

"Mrs. William James Stillman,"
Michael Stillman Collection, Roseland, N.J.

"Chaucer at the Court of Edward III,"
Municipal Art Gallery, Sydney.

"Romeo and Juliet,"
Rockford Collection, Wilmington, Del.

PIETER BRUEGEL THE ELDER. Only a few facts concerning the life of Bruegel have come down to us. A native of the borderland of what is now known as modern Holland and Belgium, Bruegel studied under Pieter Coeck van Aelst, and in 1551 entered the Guild of Painters as a master. He travelled through France and Italy and was in Rome in 1553. In 1563 the artist married the daughter of his master and had two sons who were also distinguished as artists. Bruegel died in 1569 and was buried in Notre Dame de la Chapelle at Brussels.

Bruegel's genius as a painter bridges the gap between the medieval and modern worlds. His mind was preoccupied with sacred themes as well as secular ones, and he was one of the first painters to illustrate the truths of Christianity by using contemporary persons as models. Looking at his animated crowds of peasants, the Flemish scene of four hundred years ago comes to life before our eyes, and we enter easily into the moods of the Netherlands of that time. Bruegel could be mystical, macabre and entirely joyous by contrast, as his pictures of death and devils, festivals and dances indicate. Said to have been a peasant himself, he perfectly understood the people occupied in rural pursuits. As well as being an ingenious and realistic figure-artist he was a marvellous landscape painter, and one of the first marine painters of Europe. His series of pictures of the seasons, in their atmospheric feeling for nature, are masterpieces. A universally known painting by Bruegel is the one entitled "Hunters in the Snow". This work and the equally famous "The Peasant Dance" are in the Kunsthistorisches Museum, Vienna.

A. B.

PRINCIPAL WORKS BY PIETER BRUEGEL THE ELDER

"The Dull Griet" (Mad Meg),
Musée Mayer van den Bergh, Antwerp.

"Death of the Virgin,"
National Trust, Upton House, Banbury.

"The Netherlandish Proverbs,"
Kaiser Friedriches Museum, Berlin.

"Adoration of the Kings,"
"The Fall of the Rebel Angels,"
Musées Royaux des Beaux Arts, Brussels.

"Wedding Dance in the Open Air,"
Institute of Arts, Detroit.

"The Massacre of the Innocents,"
Hampton Court Palace.

"Adoration of the Kings,"
"The Flight into Egypt,"
"Christ and the Woman taken in Adultery,"
National Gallery, London.

"Head of an old Peasant Woman,"
Bayerische Staatsgemäldesammlungen, Munich.

"The Corn Harvest,"
"Landscape with Fall of Icarus,"
Metropolitan Museum of Art, New York.

"Children's Games,"
"The Suicide of Saul,"
"The Tower of Babel,"
"The Procession to Calvary,"
"Hunters in the Snow,"
"The Peasant Dance,"
"Storm at Sea,"
Kunsthistorisches Museum, Vienna.

SIR EDWARD BURNE-JONES

1833-1898

*

KING COPHETUA AND THE BEGGAR MAID

TATE GALLERY, LONDON

BRITISH PRE-RAPHAELITE SCHOOL

King Cophetua and the Beggar Maid

THE ancient story of the king who

"cared not for women-kinde,
But did them all disdaine"

until one day he saw a lovely beggar maid with whom he fell instantly in love, and whom he made his queen, was so popular in Elizabethan times that frequent allusions thereto are made by the dramatists: Ben Jonson in *Every Man in his Humour* among them; and Shakespeare in no less than four of his plays, as where Mercutio refers in *Romeo and Juliet* to

"Cupid, he that shot so trim,
When King Cophetua loved the beggar maid."

Which derives directly from the old ballad on the subject preserved by Bishop Percy in his *Reliques of Ancient English Poetry:*

"The blinded boy, that shootes so trim,
From Heaven down did hie
He drew a dart and shot at him,
In place where he did lie."

Burne-Jones has caught the spirit of the old lay and treated it as romance should be treated, with all the beauty and tenderness at his command. The moment chosen is that in which the monarch has brought his love to the palace in her humble dress and set her on his throne—the moment that Tennyson chose for his lyric "The Beggar Maid":

"As shines the moon in clouded skies,
She in her poor attire was seen:
One praised her ancles, one her eyes,
One her dark hair and lovesome mien.
So sweet a face, such angel grace,
In all that land had never been:
Cophetua sware a royal oath:
'This beggar maid shall be my queen!' "

C. R. C.